Creative
Visualization

Creative Visualization

to attain your goals
and improve your well-being

Nevill Drury

Barnes & Noble Books
BOOKS
NEW YORK

Contents

Introduction

During a public address in Sydney just prior to the 2000 Olympic Games, Nelson Mandela made this observation: 'One of the most difficult things is not to change society, but to change ourselves.' Although changing ourselves is certainly a challenge, we can do much to help ourselves – whether we are considering our physical health, our mental well-being, or even our spiritual perspectives. Each of us can take the responsibility for transforming our own lives and, in so doing, assist the development and transformation of the society in which we live, and eventually the world as a whole.

If we are to do this, we require a vision for our own individual lives. We need to be able to envision how we are now and where we are headed in the future, on all levels of our individual awareness. This is where creative visualization can play a key role, because it is through our powers of imagination that we are able to conceive of a different and better future for ourselves and those who are important to us. It is through our powers of imagination that we are able to focus our creative resources in order to bring into reality those things we need to make our life more fulfilled and more productive.

When we talk of 'visualization,' we mean focusing the potentials and resources of our mind through the use of visual imagery. When we visualize, we draw on imagery from both the conscious and unconscious parts of our mind, and we do this in different ways. First, we do it through memory, by drawing on sensory impressions from the everyday world. Second, we do it through each of our senses, and this helps our inner world to come alive. Third, we do it through the organising ability of our mind, which provides us with visual images that have meaning. And finally, we do it through our emotions, which help us engage with the images we are seeing in our 'mind's eye.'

Creative visualization can help us accomplish important tasks, to overcome personal barriers created by the beliefs we hold, as well as to relate positively to the symptoms of disease.

All of this means that our creative imagination provides us with a wonderful transformative resource; it is up to us to draw upon its seemingly infinite potential. Creative visualization can help us attain our goals, and actually become who and what we wish to be.

Exploring Our Imagination

What do we mean by 'imagination?'

Although some of us claim to be more 'imaginative' or 'visually oriented' than others, we all use the powers of our imagination much more than we realize! We communicate with one another primarily by using words, and words themselves are vitally important in everyday life for this reason alone. However, it is worth remembering that we actually *think* in images. Most words we use in our everyday communications have a direct connection with specific images.

We enter the world of our imagination when we daydream or fantasize, when we think about things that happened in the past, or when we visualize the sorts of things we would like to achieve or obtain in the future. We are also using our powers of imagination when we summon with our mind's eye the visual image of someone we know personally, or when we recall a particular sensory impression that has been stored in our memory.

As an aspect of conscious awareness, creative visualization is of course performed in the brain, so it will be helpful in the first instance to consider the two different aspects of the brain – the left and right hemispheres – and the different types of function that each hemisphere contributes to our thought processes.

The left and right brain hemispheres

The pioneering neurophysiologists of the nineteenth century did not distinguish between the left and right hemispheres, regarding the brain as an essentially uniform mass, with all parts of the brain playing an equal role in its effective functioning. However, following the investigations of brain researchers such as Roger Sperry and Robert Ornstein, we now know that the brain itself seems to divide into two sections, each dealing with different types of thought.

The left hemisphere of the brain is associated with analytical and logical thought, with verbal and written communication, and with mathematical concepts. The right hemisphere deals with spatial relationships and with wholes rather than with parts; that is to say, its emphasis is on holistic (or wholistic) thinking rather than linear or sequential analysis. When we list the different functions of the right and left and brain hemispheres, they include the following:

Our left brain is associated with:

+ the right side of the body
+ linear processing of information
+ our awareness of the passage of time
+ reading, writing and verbal expression
+ mathematical functions and calculations
+ logic and reason
+ analysis

Our right brain is associated with:

+ the left side of the body
+ our sense of space and rhythm
+ our intuitions and emotions
+ our sensitivity, passion and creativity
+ visual imagery and dreams
+ synthesis

Because it utilizes visual imagery, creative visualization draws primarily on the right hemisphere of the brain. For this reason, creative visualization is an approach to developing conscious awareness which many people believe could be more effectively applied in everyday life. It is widely acknowledged that in our so-called 'developed' Western society, which in turn is dominated by scientific thinking, computers, and advanced technology, we have developed our left brain at the expense of our right. Some critics of the modern Western lifestyle believe we rely far too much on linear thought, on processing information step by step through different stages, causing us to pay too little attention to our powers of intuition and creativity. Expressed more poetically, we in the West operate far too much through our heads and not enough through our hearts. What we probably all need to do is blend aspects of both brain hemispheres more effectively. Developing our powers of creative visualization can help us do this.

How do we perceive?

All human beings have evolved in a similar manner, using the physical senses to respond to the world and to other human beings in much the same way, through language and gestures. If this were not the case, we would never be able to communicate with one another! Each of us has eyes that receive radiant electromagnetic energy, ears that tune into vibrations in the air, a nose that contains receptors for gaseous molecules, specific touch sensors, and a range of cells on the tongue that respond to molecules in food and provide us with our sense of taste.

As we continue to experience the sensory overload of modern daily life, our brain actually helps us remain coherent and 'normal' by filtering out a lot of the sensory input that we don't need. For example, the eye transmits less than one trillionth of the information reaching its surface, so a massive difference exists between the available sensory data impinging on the eyeball and what the brain subsequently constructs as our 'consensus reality': the world we perceive and share with others. We see the way we see, and agree on our shared experiences with other human beings, because we have all evolved with comparable faculties of perception and comparable filtering systems.

If it is true that so many of us living in the West are letting our left-brain functions dominate the right side of our brain, then it follows that we are only fulfilling half of our potential as human beings. Creative visualization helps us integrate both sides of the brain, perhaps even producing intuitive solutions to mathematical problems. A well-known and often quoted example of this

type of brain function is provided by the case of the German chemist Friedrich Kekulé (1829–96). Kekulé had been pondering on the structure of the benzene molecule, drawing essentially on his powers of intellectual and analytic thought. Sitting beside his fire at home, he began to doze off, and while in a half-sleeping state, he pictured a snake with its tail in its mouth! This image startled him so much that he awoke. The image of the snake, however, had provided him with an insight into the structure of benzene, which consists of a ring of six carbon atoms, giving him a visual solution to the specific intellectual problem with which he had been grappling. Kekulé had been using his left brain in the first instance, but it was his right brain that provided him with his answer! This brings home the point that creativity draws not only on logic and reason, but also on the non-verbal, picture-making faculties of the right brain hemisphere.

As we will see, all our senses play a role in our imagination, but creative visualization means focusing primarily on the visual and emotional dimensions of the imagination, since these are the areas of creative awareness that have most to do with achieving our personal aims.

The power of visual images

We can think of the imagination as the brain's capacity to create images of objects and situations that are not objectively real or directly available to the senses. Obviously, what we call 'imagination' is an internal process. The mind produces images by drawing on memory to create impressions of people and events. However, while these images are often visual, they are sometimes associated with other senses as well. It is possible for the mind to create images of sound, images of movement, images relating to touch, as well as images associated with smell, pain, or temperature. When we practice creative visualization, we will deal mostly with visual images simply because, for most people, these types of images are the most familiar and the most effective.

A fascinating and very important thing about images is that they can lead to an emotional or bodily response. This means that if you imagine yourself in a hypothetical situation, and hold this image in your mind's eye *as if it were real*, you will create a result in your body that is consistent with the image itself. It does not matter at all in this context whether the image is 'real' or produced through your powers of creative visualization. If the image is strong and convincing, it will create a tangible result. If you *believe* it is real, it will have just as much impact as the real thing.

Creativity combines reason and logic with the formation of images. Image creation is a function of the right-brain hemisphere, but reason and logic derive from the left brain. So in creative visualization, we are bringing both brain functions together in order to expand the horizons of our personal awareness.

Attuning ourselves to our senses

Some people claim that they are not especially gifted visually, that they don't see pictorial images when they close their eyes and enter the inner world we associate with the imagination. However, unless we were born blind at birth, each one of us has the potential to create visual images, even if we have got out of practice and lost the knack for doing so. We all need to hone and utilize our powers of visualization in much the same way that we need to exercise our physical limbs in order to stay fit and healthy. One way to start doing this is by focusing on each of the senses in turn.

Let's begin by identifying each of the particular senses – sight, smell, touch, taste, hearing, and movement.

Begin by sitting in a comfortable position, closing your eyes and relaxing. Now switch your attention completely to *seeing* – focusing all your powers of inner awareness on one of the following items:

- ❖ a golden sun
- ❖ a silver crescent moon
- ❖ a blue circle
- ❖ a red triangle
- ❖ a colorful bird flying through the air

Did you notice any bodily sensation as you focused on these images? In yoga meditation, a silver moon is a symbol of water, a blue circle is a symbol of air, and a red triangle is a symbol of fire. Did these specific visual images provoke any associated sensations? What color was the bird? Was it an exotic, unfamiliar species or a bird you have seen frequently in your garden?

Did you pay attention to the rich colors of its feathers, or the color of its eyes and beak? How specifically did you really see this bird?

Now try concentrating on *smell*. Begin by imagining those smells that appeal to you and also those that repel you, bringing them all as fully as you can into your conscious awareness. Experience the intoxicating scent of a beautiful rose or a cluster of purple violets. Alternatively, focus on the delicious smell of freshly baked bread or a freshly peeled mandarin, or any other aroma you find enticing. Now try to recall the decidedly unpleasant smell of a carton of moldy yogurt that you have discovered lurking at the back of your refrigerator! Focusing occasionally on negative images can be good practice as well.

Next, concentrate on your sense of *touch*. Imagine in your mind's eye that you are running your fingers across someone else's skin. Feel the softness and perhaps also the wrinkles, the little bumps and grooves, the textures that make the surface of the skin so distinctive. Now imagine stroking your hand through soft snow, under running water, or across smooth, warm sand. What impressions come to mind as you do this? Do any particular associations emerge from your store of personal memories?

Now focus your awareness on your sense of *taste*. Recall that delicious cup of tea or coffee, or that scrumptious muffin that you had at breakfast, or the distinctive taste of a particular type of fruit juice or alcoholic beverage that you really enjoyed on a recent occasion. Feel the taste on your lips.

Turn your attention to your sense of *hearing*. Listen to the distinctive song of a bird outside in the garden, or concentrate on the qualities of a particular person's voice. Recall the delightful sound of a golden trumpet playing a favorite melody, or the distinctive sound of bells chiming in a village church or cathedral. What is it that makes these sounds so distinctive? Do any of these

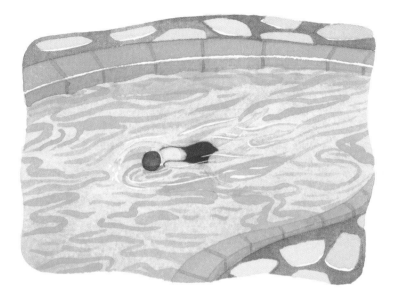

sounds evoke a particular emotional resonance for you? Are any of them associated with a particular memory?

Finally, focus your conscious awareness on your sense of *movement*. In your mind's eye, imagine first that you are walking, then that you are running, and finally that you are dancing. Now visualize yourself swimming in a pool, or driving a car. Feel that sense of movement as you visualize these activities. Imagine how it feels to really be there.

As we gradually become attuned to summoning specific images and sensory impressions into our field of awareness, we can in turn focus on other ways of enhancing how real they then become for us. This in turn will produce real benefits as we learn to focus our attention on our personal goals or specific milestones on our individual path toward fulfillment and well-being. The important thing to remember is that in the world of creative visualization, our thoughts create our reality. What we truly believe really can come true.

First Steps in Creative Visualization

First principles

One of the basic principles underlying the practice of creative visualization is that each of us can become what we aspire to be. The only barriers limiting our potential are those we impose upon ourselves through the restraints of our imagination. After all, what we believe about ourselves defines the territory for our personal development. We can fence ourselves in with negative or restrictive belief systems and concepts, or we can seek options in our lives that are liberating, transforming, and empowering.

The second of these two options is what creative visualization is all about. With effort, what we envision for our lives will ultimately become true for us in our everyday experience. Creative visualization works because the mind accepts beliefs as being real. So if we can use the techniques of creative visualization to align our beliefs about ourselves with our personal goals, we will certainly be heading in the right direction. Another way of saying this is that if our beliefs are positive, we will probably have a positive experience of life. On the other hand, if our beliefs are negative, we will probably have a negative experience of life. Once again, we must emphasize the key point: *our thoughts help create our reality*.

Imagination is like a flow of energy

Increasingly, people who practice creative visualization come to regard pure consciousness – the very act of being aware – as the most central fact of our existence. We learn to move beyond the limitations of our beliefs and our concepts about ourselves while defining our personal goals more specifically. We also learn to use our imagination to dissolve personal boundaries and to remove the obstacles getting in the way of who we are and who we wish to become. The core truth of this can easily be demonstrated. When you close your eyes to meditate or to concentrate on a visual image, it is your inner world that becomes your central experience – and this inner world has no limitations.

According to the Eastern spiritual traditions of yoga and Buddhism, your state of consciousness determines your perceptual reality, and the more you expand your personal horizons, the more limitless your potential becomes. The mind speaks to us in images; the way we learn to transform our awareness through our response to imagery will help us live our lives more effectively. We can think of our individual lives and our personal response to everyday reality as being like a stream of energy. As with a flowing river, we can erect obstacles or barriers to deflect the flow, not unlike the barriers of our personal belief systems, or the restrictions caused by our negative thoughts about ourselves.

Creative visualization teaches us to literally go with the flow, opening ourselves to the tide of new possibilities. We learn to heed our intuitions and respect the visual imagery that our mind presents to us. In turn, we can respond to our mind by using the powers of our imagination to imprint goals and aspirations defining who and what we wish to become.

So creative visualization is very much a two-way process. We speak to our mind in images, and it in turn speaks back to us in images, like the ebb and flow of a tide. Imagination is like a flow of energy. We can learn to influence, and be shaped by, the limitless potentials presented to us through our use of creative visualization.

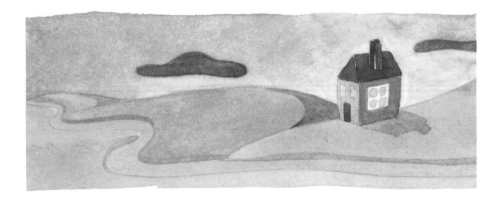

Visualizing specific goals

When it comes to using the creative power of your imagination
to obtain what you want, three key things should be remembered:

- You must be able to visualize the desired object or situation clearly
- You must believe that what you visualize will actually happen
- You must visualize the end result as if it has come to pass, rather
  than just focus on the means of obtaining it

Successful creative visualization requires developing clear goals and precise
targets. Once you have established a clear goal, you must develop a mind-set
affirming that you are now unstoppable in your pursuit of that goal. It also
helps if you can feel good about the pursuit of your goal; that
adds a depth to your sense of purpose. Meanwhile, the goal
or target then becomes a focus for your mind; if your mind
accepts the goal, all your creativity and personal
motivation will be aroused to help you achieve that
particular goal. Maybe you are looking for a specific
promotion at work, or perhaps you have seen a new car and
are seeking to motivate yourself to save
enough money to buy it? Or maybe you have a
particular relationship in mind; for example, a
specific person you would like to get to know
better in order to develop what you hope will
become a close relationship. You must be able to
hold in your mind's eye the specific details of that
new job or car, see yourself interacting closely with that
special person, and visualize these details with great
conviction, so that these positive thoughts then have the
opportunity to manifest for you as real events in your life.

Having said that, it is important to also acknowledge that your aspirations must be potentially attainable, otherwise what you are striving for is based on fantasy, delusion, or make-believe.

In the examples mentioned above, you have to actually have the potential to hold the job in question, the motivation to put money aside, or the actual possibility of a loving and caring relationship with the person whom you are visualizing as a partner. Wishing for something to happen out of sheer desperation when the odds are stacked against you is not what creative visualization is about. Creative visualization is about overcoming obstacles to make what is potentially possible actually happen.

Obviously, some goals are relatively easy to achieve while others require much more effort. *Hoping* for a specific outcome is fine, provided that hope is based on a real possibility. That hope also has to be converted into a positive conviction that what is hoped for will actually come to pass. If at some deep inner level we are unsure about our goal, we will probably end up sabotaging our particular quest; our creative visualization won't work, because deep down we don't really believe that the target is attainable. The more convinced we are about the outcome, the more likely our creative visualization will bring it to pass.

Overcoming the limits of our beliefs

We have already discussed the idea that what we believe about something holds the key to attaining it, and that the only barriers limiting our potential are those we impose upon ourselves through the restraints of our imagination. In one of his recent books Wayne Dyer makes an interesting distinction between believing something and knowing something.

'Beliefs restrict you,' says Dyer, but 'knowings empower you.' The task here is to convert what you *believe* can happen into what you know can happen. Knowing that something can really happen then imprints itself on your consciousness, removing any hint of doubt about the outcome. If any doubt were to linger, it would become a limitation that could easily build into a major obstacle. Dyer thinks that we should seek to convert our beliefs into knowings, which will greatly assist us when fears, obstacles, and traumas enter our lives.

Making a plan of action

Often, supplementing your creative visualizations with a plan of action can prove helpful in defining your goal more specifically and enhancing the effectiveness of your visualizations.

The idea is to make a personal sketch or drawing of your plan of action. Take a standard sheet of paper, and make a hand-drawn border around it. This is your way of defining the task at hand. Make a circle at the top of the sheet of paper, preferably in the center, labeling this as the goal you are setting out to achieve. Now make another mark at the corresponding location at the 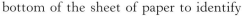 bottom of the sheet of paper to identify where you are now. Obviously, the idea is to chart your plan of action from the present moment through to actually achieving the goal you have set yourself. Think of all the stages that are required to achieve the outcome, along with all the additional tasks you will have to undertake to achieve this goal. These details will take up most of the space in the center of your sketch – between the starting point at the bottom and the successful outcome identified at the top.

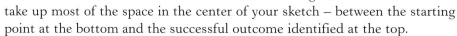

For example, let's consider a situation in which you wish to prepare a special report on a subject that you find quite demanding. You are nevertheless fascinated by the particular topic. The report will involve some interviews with specialists in the field, which you will find interesting, but challenging. You are a little anxious about successfully producing the report because you are not entirely confident about this undertaking. However, deep down you feel the task is within the range of your abilities.

Preparing this report will involve several different activities, and a logical and well-planned course of action. You will have to make special trips to the college library, track down some obscure reference books and magazine articles, put time aside to use the Internet, as well as arrange interviews with a number of key people whose views are important for your report. Then you will have to allocate time for typing transcripts of the interviews and checking back with your interviewees to ensure that you have described their views correctly. Finally, you will have to prepare a number of drafts of your report until you arrive at a final version with which you are happy. You will also have to make notes on your personal social commitments with friends and family at all the various stages of this undertaking, to ensure that the time frame for the various components of your plan is realistic. All these individual stages and activities can be written down on your plan of action, supplemented with creative visualizations in which you see yourself as a confident person who has successfully mastered each of these interactions. By the time you have completed your plan of action, you will find that you have detailed a number of specific but interconnected activities, all leading to the final desired outcome. In your final visualization, you will see yourself as a competent person who has completed a report that is well received by all who read it.

When you assess your plan of action, you will notice something interesting: your plan is a whole (represented by the single sheet of paper), but it consists of several logical steps and stages, all of which are necessary to achieve a successful outcome and take place in a particular time sequence. Your plan overall is a whole (right hemisphere), but its constituent components take place in a logical sequence occuring within a particular time frame (left hemisphere). So in producing your plan of action, you have drawn on both the right and left hemispheres of your brain to focus on what you expect to achieve as the final result. Your plan of action helps reinforce your creative visualizations of achieving something you already know is possible.

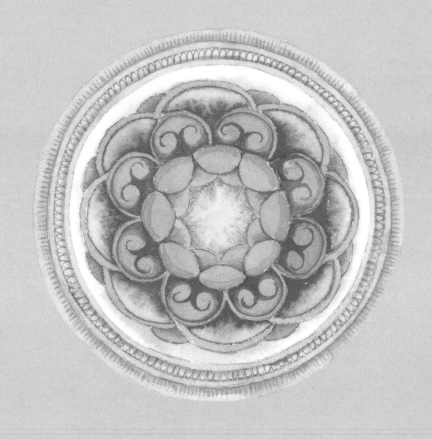

The future belongs to those who believe in their dreams

Relaxation and Positive Affirmations

Learning to relax

Most people find that the best way to begin practicing creative visualization is by learning first of all how to relax. There are many ways of doing this, and you will have to find a way that works for you. Two different approaches are described below. The important point to remember is that relaxation provides us with a sense of openness and inner stillness that allows us to center our awareness. Once we have achieved this sense of feeling focused and fully aware, we can concentrate on our specific goals and positive affirmations.

Tension is incompatible with relaxation. When we relax our body and our mind, we automatically reduce the tension that tightens our muscles. This is how relaxation exercises actually reduce stress and anxiety, and produce a feeling of well-being. Once you've learned how your muscles should feel when they are relaxed, it then becomes a matter of regular practice to bring them into that relaxed state.

The first muscle relaxation technique described here will show you how to induce deep muscular relaxation by tensing and then releasing tension from various parts of your body, one section at a time.

TENSE-AND-RELEASE MUSCLE RELAXATION

This is a well-proven technique of muscle relaxation based on the research of the Chicago physician Edmund Jacobson. Jacobson did his basic research in the 1920s, but his approach still provides the basis for most forms of relaxation training practiced today. You can either memorize the main steps in this muscle relaxation technique or ask a friend to read this text aloud to you as you relax in a comfortable chair and follow the procedures step by step:

❖ *Lean back in your chair. Make yourself comfortable.*
Place both of your feet flat on the floor.
Rest your hands comfortably in your lap.

❖ *Begin by stretching your legs as far as they can go ... Relax.*
Stretch your legs again.
Move your feet up, toward you ...
Turn your feet down, away from you ... Hold ...
Relax ...

❖ *Now, tighten the muscles in your calves and those in your thighs.*
Hold tight, hold tight ... and relax ...

❖ *Allow your legs to return slowly to their original position, relaxing all the*
muscles in your feet, all the muscles in your calves, then all the muscles in
your thighs.
Relax your legs completely.
Now take a few moments to experience that wonderful sense of relaxation
coming up from your calves and your thighs.
Remain relaxed and calm ... very relaxed ... calm and relaxed ...
Focus on your legs and experience that feeling of relaxation.

❖ *Now stretch out your arms.*
Make two fists and tighten the muscles in your fingers.
Feel the tightness ... Hold tight, hold tight ... and now relax.
Allow your arms to return to their resting position. Experience that relaxation.
Now stretch your arms again.
Tighten the muscles in your wrists, in your lower arms, then in your
upper arms ...
Hold tight, hold tight ... and now let go, let go ... allowing your arms to
return to their original position.
Now stop for a few moments, taking the opportunity to experience that
wonderful feeling of relaxation coming into your fingers, into your hands,
then flowing through to your lower and upper arms ...

❖ *Allow your arms to become competely limp.*
Reflect once again on that feeling of deep relaxation that you are now experiencing.
You are now feeling very relaxed and very calm ... very relaxed and very calm.

❖ *Next, arch your back and raise your chest.*
Tighten the muscles in your chest, your abdomen, your back and your neck.
Hold it ... hold it ... and now let go of the tension ... let go of the tension.
Notice how your muscles relax. Take a few moments to experience your muscles relaxing in your chest, in your abdomen, in your neck ... and all across your back. Notice that all your muscles now feel nicely relaxed.

❖ *Try tightening the muscles in your face ... first the muscles around your forehead ... then the muscles around your eyes. Make them tighter. Hold it ... hold it ... and now relax.*
Now tighten the muscles of your cheeks, the muscles around your mouth, the muscles of your chin. Make them tighter ... Hold it, hold it ... and relax.

❖ *Now allow all the muscles in your face to relax ... first the muscles in your chin ... then the muscles around your mouth ... the muscles of your cheeks ... the muscles around your eyes ... the muscles of your forehead.*
Allow any tension to drain away from your face.
You can also allow your chin to sag if that feels good.
Take a few moments to enjoy that feeling of relaxation.
You are feeling very relaxed and very calm ... very relaxed and very calm.

❧ Next, breathe in through your nose, slowly and deeply.
First breathe the air deep down into your abdomen, then into your chest,
and finally allow it to rise into your throat.
Hold it, hold it ... and slowly breathe it out through your nose.
Experience that feeling of relaxation.
Breathe in, tense up ... Breathe out, relax ...

❧ Once again, take a very deep breath, hold it ... hold it, and slowly let it out.
Let go of all your tension – together with any frustrations, any anxieties
you are experiencing – as you feel more and more relaxed ... more relaxed
and calm ...

❧ Now take a few moments to do a full scan of your body.
If you become aware of any tense area that still remains in your body,
take time to release that tension.
And still you are feeling calm and relaxed ... calm and relaxed.

❧ Finally, take a few moments simply to breathe in and out a few times and
stretch your body.
Focus once more on your immediate surroundings.
You are now preparing to return to your daily activities.
Stay relaxed and calm.
Remain focused and attentive ... the new day is yours!

Another, simpler method ...

Another approach to relaxation that I have personally found helpful as a prelude to creative visualization involves what is sometimes known as progressive relaxation. It is a simpler form of the procedure outlined above. In this approach, you don't actually tense up different parts of your body and then relax them; instead, you simply visualize the different parts of your body becoming progressively relaxed in sequence. Try this method if you find the tense-and-relax technique too involved. This simpler approach also has the advantage that you can remember the basic visualization yourself, and you won't have to ask someone else to read out the steps to you.

SIMPLE RELAXATION

Sit comfortably on the floor or in a chair, loosen any items of clothing that are likely to provide distraction or discomfort, then begin progressively to relax different parts of your body. You might like to begin by visualizing that your feet are now becoming increasingly limp and relaxed, then your ankles and your calves have also relaxed. Imagine now that your legs are completely relaxed and that a soothing feeling of relaxation has entered your abdomen and is working its way into your upper body, stage by stage. Now your chest is becoming completely relaxed, and you are breathing deeply and without restriction. Finally, relax your arms, allowing the focus of your attention to remain solely in your head. Your focus should remain on awareness itself, for from this point onwards your emphasis will be on summoning into your field of vision those specific images that are part of your creative visualization.

Is creative visualization like meditation?

Creative visualization is sometimes called 'active meditation,' or 'seeing with the mind's eye.' Many familiar forms of Eastern meditation involve eliminating imagery from consciousness altogether, thereby removing the distractions provided by the chatter of the mind. Meditation is sometimes described as an act of letting go: letting go of the limitations of the body, the mind, and the emotions. However, although creative visualization can be regarded as a form of meditation, it has a somewhat different emphasis. Rather than negating visual imagery, it involves summoning into our sphere of perception specific images helpful in providing insights and solutions that relate directly to personal issues in our life.

Creative visualization teaches us to use the powers of our imagination to find out more about ourselves, to solve problems we may be experiencing, and to change those entrenched attitudes and beliefs that we continue to hold on to as the very cornerstones of our existence. Creative visualization also allows us to use the potentials of our imagination in order to anticipate change and to envision different outcomes.

As we have already emphasized, an important principle of creative visualization is to engage with the images that arise into consciousness *as if they were real*. Creative visualization involves summoning images into consciousness in such a way that they have a three-dimensional presence, and are both convincing and alive within our spectrum of awareness. When we practice creative visualization, we are drawing on images and impressions from our memories, from our senses, from our emotions, and from the deepest and most spiritual regions of our minds. One way of making creative images more real is to literally breathe life into them.

The breath of life

Controlled breathing is an important adjunct to creative visualization; the two go hand in hand. It becomes highly effective, for example, to visualize the flow of breath as a rejuvenating force sustaining the whole body.

One of the best breathing techniques to use is the so-called Abdominal Breath, which involves reversing our familiar breathing habits. Most of us breathe by breathing in, lifting our chest and caving in the stomach. What we really should be doing when we breathe is pushing down our diaphragm, filling the lower part of the lungs, and then making the stomach balloon out. As we breathe out, our stomach will then sink in again and our diaphragm will return to its original position. This rhythm of controlled breathing is widely used in yoga to attain greater energy and a heightened sense of centeredness.

Opposite is a visualization that is useful as you practice controlled breathing.

Remember, the way we breathe is affected by our thoughts and our feelings. If we are happy, we breathe more freely and easily. If we are anxious or tense, our breathing can be shallow, hesitant, or uneven. This leads us to another important aspect of creative visualization: the act of staying positive.

VISUALIZE YOUR BREATHING

Visualize your breath as a stream of white light that enters the crown of your head, then spirals down through your body like a vortex. Watch your breath as it spirals down into different parts of your body – your throat, your chest, your abdomen, your arms and legs – and imagine that it is revitalizing each part of your body in turn, filling each organ with oxygen and life force. You may also find it helpful to visualize this vortex of white light surging through your blood capillaries, helping each organ function effectively, literally bringing each part of your body to life.

At the same time, concentrate on the rhythm of your breath as air enters your body and is then expelled. Build your breathing up gradually so it becomes stronger and more focused. Don't allow your mind to wander or create any distractions. If you find that your powers of concentration are wavering, bring your focus back to the essential in–out rhythm of your breathing and the spiralling vortex of light. In this way, you will stay fully centered, truly 'at one' with yourself.

Positive affirmations

Because thoughts originate in our inner world, they often have an intangible quality that is hard to pin down. However, it is worth reflecting on how our mind constructs our thoughts as part of our conscious and unconscious experience of the world and our place in it. That many of the diseases in modern society spring directly from what we think and the way we feel about ourselves is hardly surprising. For this reason, when we practice creative visualization, it is a good idea to focus on the positive rather than the negative, to visualize what we actually want rather than what we don't want. We can do this by making positive affirmations.

Affirmations are concise, accurate statements describing our goals. The most effective affirmations are those you create yourself that draw on your own knowledge and experience. An affirmation is essentially a positive statement that you make to yourself in order to strengthen and reinforce your beliefs. It can relate to yourself, to other people, or to any issue of personal concern.

The essential characteristics of affirmations are as follows:

- ⁜ They must be written in the first person
- ⁜ They must be in the present tense
- ⁜ They must relate directly to your personal goal
- ⁜ They should be positive
- ⁜ They should be specific, accurate and realistic
- ⁜ They should be powerfully expressed and convincing
- ⁜ They should contain words with good personal associations

Affirmations only work if you are truly willing to integrate the goals expressed in the affirmation, both within your personality and also in everyday life. You can repeat your affirmations several times a day on a regular basis, write them down, or express them out loud. With time, the positive statement you are making in your affirmation will begin to describe how you really are, and will not feel like an attitude superimposed from outside.

Affirmations should begin with the words 'I am' or 'I have'; they should indicate that the goal has already been achieved. The essential aim is to give the mind a target that it can lock on to. For example: 'I am a successful person now.'

Here are some other examples of positive affirmations:

- *I am a friendly and outgoing person*
- *I am calm and even-tempered*
- *I am arranging my daily business schedules efficiently*
- *I give and receive love freely*
- *I am an open channel of spiritual energy*

You may also find it helpful to combine silent affirmations with the deep-breathing technique we referred to earlier. Breathe into your abdomen, hold your breath as you mentally repeat your affirmation, then breathe out, feeling as you do so that your affirmation has enriched all aspects of your physical and emotional well-being.

Well-known consciousness researcher Shakti Gawain believes that all effective affirmations have three important elements: *desire* (you must truly want to change); *belief* (you must believe that change is possible); and *acceptance* (you must be willing to have the change take place). In the next chapter, we will describe how we can formulate our goals by using creative visualization and positive affirmations in a variety of specific contexts and situations.

Personal Goals and Aspirations

Manifesting

When we create positive affirmations, we are assuming that we are already in the situation in which we want to be. It is not a matter of *wishing* we could achieve something: we have to visualize ourselves totally, completely and convincingly *in* that particular situation. By doing this, we are bringing the future into the present, opening ourselves to the possibility of change.

It may sound obvious, but the key skill here is focusing our awareness on attracting into our lives those things that we really want. Sometimes, this process is called 'manifestation.' Creative visualization and positive affirmations are both ways of manifesting.

Visualization creates a specific picture in our mind; positive affirmations trigger new thought processes that can help us overcome earlier mental programming that may be holding us back.

What do you really want?

When we are establishing our personal priorities, what things come first to mind? Are we seeking financial prosperity and material security – a better-paying job, a bigger house, a new car? Are we focusing primarily on our personal relationships with others – our wives, husbands, lovers, friends, parents or children? Are we preoccupied with issues of self-esteem and recognition – wanting to receive more respect and acknowledgement from our family, friends and peers, or an even broader scale of recognition involving national or international fame? These may be some of the things that come to mind as we assess our most deeply felt priorities in life.

As we have seen, the essential purpose of creative visualization is to envision positive outcomes, then to make them manifest in our everyday lives. And these outcomes can be on any level we choose to focus on. The outcomes we seek can be purely physical, involving, for example, the acquisition of

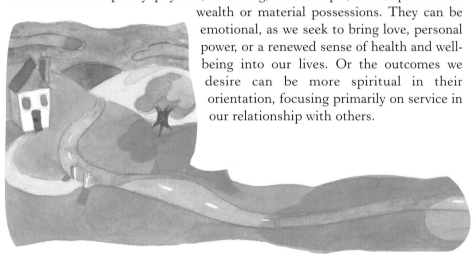

wealth or material possessions. They can be emotional, as we seek to bring love, personal power, or a renewed sense of health and well-being into our lives. Or the outcomes we desire can be more spiritual in their orientation, focusing primarily on service in our relationship with others.

Listing your personal goals

You can begin by making an inventory of your own personal goals and aspirations.

Write them down in a list: 'Things I would like to change in my life'

1. _____
2. _____
3. _____
4. _____
5. _____
6. _____ etc.

Now make yourself a plan of action for each of these personal goals, starting with where you are right now and where you want to finish up with regard to each personal goal or aspiration on your list. If your goal is an ongoing one, you may like to consider specific stages of progress on a time scale – where you want to be in one year, in two years, in five years – and so on. The next step will be to write positive affirmations for the main stages of your plan of action, then to practice creative visualizations in which you see yourself achieving each of these stages in turn, on the path to success.

Material goals

These are the most obvious and specific. Let's say you have the goal of buying a new, bright red MG sports car in one year's time. You will need to make a detailed plan of action relating to where you will find such a car, how you will put money aside to pay for it, what sorts of terms will be involved in that payment, and so on. When you have done this, create affirmations focusing specifically on attaining this particular car, not a white one or a silver one, or any other model. Stick with your vision for attaining this particular goal. Do not deviate unless a genuine reason for changing your mind presents itself.

Love and relationships

You can also establish goals which focus on your love life and personal relationships. What is the specific kind of relationship you are seeking? Do you want to have children? If so, how many, and with whom? What sort of family life do you envision for yourself? If it is friends you are seeking, how many good friendships do you really want? With all your present commitments, how many friends do you really have time for? And what are you really seeking from these new friends? Would such a relationship truly be a two-way process of both giving and receiving? In what ways would you interact with these new friends to demonstrate your commitment to them?

Educational and professional goals

It may be that you intend to take further training or classes to expand your personal knowledge or gain further qualifications. What are your specific goals or aspirations in this area of your life? How long will these courses take you, and what are the various stages involved? What sort of job do you envision for yourself at the completion of your studies? How will your new profession or position be more rewarding and fulfilling for you?

Perhaps you are also experiencing a certain amount of anxiety about a job interview for an important position. Your visualization may involve imagining the room and people where the interview is taking place, your confident responses to questions put to you by the interviewing panel, and your being offered the position.

Health and well-being

Perhaps you have some specific health problems and you are setting yourself goals in these areas. Are you overweight or unfit, do you have a blood cholesterol problem involving a change of diet, or are there specific allergies which you have to treat? Do you wish to overcome bad habits such as laziness or lethargy? Again, you can make a plan of action for your personal goals, accompanying them with positive affirmations and visualizations in which you see yourself shedding former bad habits or unhealthy dietary practices, becoming increasingly well and healthy through a series of targeted stages.

Spiritual goals

You may wish to pursue a spiritual purpose in your life, becoming a volunteer or charity worker for a particular organization, or you may wish to make a firm commitment to a particular spiritual path. Perhaps you wish to start a regular pattern of keeping a dream diary so you can chart the messages sent to you from your unconscious mind? What do all these specific goals entail? Again, each of these specific activities can be systematized with a plan of action and with affirmations and creative visualizations in which you see yourself successfully participating in those activities that interest you.

One thing to remember, however, is that in areas involving emotional relationships and spiritual goals – areas in which other people are involved – you should make your affirmations and visualizations specific to what you yourself wish to achieve. Your visualizations and affirmations should not focus on what you expect from other people, because this really involves what you wish could happen, and you are not necessarily in a position to determine such an outcome. You may well be dealing here not so much with goals but with wishes about other people that may not come true – and that, in turn, could lead to great disappointment and even resentment.

Changing unwanted habits

Most people have a bad habit or two that they would like to eliminate. Maybe you are too lazy to make the bed each morning when you get up (after all, it is only going to get messed up again tomorrow!). Maybe you have an insatiable appetite for cakes, ice cream and cookies, or other delectable items, and as a consequence you are becoming seriously overweight. You know that eating these things is a bad habit, but you don't know how to shake it off (maybe, secretly, you don't want to). Or perhaps you would really like to give up smoking, as you are aware of the serious health hazards associated with smoking and would prefer not to die from lung cancer. But you don't really know how to shake off your habit, so you continue to smoke 20 or 30 cigarettes a day, at the same time reassuring yourself that in the past you used to smoke twice this number!

Some people try to change their bad habits by frightening themselves. Most of us know people who have died from cancer, or from heart attacks brought on by obesity. One response, when we hear bad news like this, is to react straight away by setting up a fitness regime – jogging enthusiastically each day, switching across to health foods and a low-fat diet. The only problem is that these changes may be superficial – they may be occurring only on the external level. Deep down, we may still be saying to ourselves: 'I know I am a smoker, a few cigarettes won't hurt,' 'I have a sweet tooth – I can't help it if I like sweet things,' or 'I can't stand jogging, it's too much like hard work, and it's no fun at all.' When this situation occurs, a clear conflict between the inner world of personal beliefs and the outer world of action exists.

Our inner world of personal beliefs is shaped by years of specific experiences and responses, which has gradually built up a picture of who we are and what we can achieve. And so, although dramatic changes of behavior in the physical world may seem like a good idea, they are doomed to failure unless they are also supported by a change in the internal world of our personal beliefs. Therefore, in order to get rid of unwanted habits (your actions), you will have to change your beliefs (your thoughts). Here is a plan of action for your unwanted habits:

First, identify the problem. You probably already know what it is: your laziness, your obesity, your smoking cigarettes, etc.

Next, identify the solution. This means setting goals for yourself, and possibly identifying various stages for scaling down your use of something that is causing damage or doing harm.

Then you have to choose between these first two options. Would you rather continue the way you have been all these years, or are you now making a conscious decision to change – to discard your old habit?

Finally. if you have decided to make the change and eliminate your bad habit, you need to imprint your decision both externally (through actions) and internally (by changing your beliefs). Internal imprinting is where creative visualization and positive affirmations play a crucial role. Your task will be to create positive emotions to support your decision for change.

Some of your affirmations may include the following:

- *I can choose new beliefs and make them part of who I am*
- *My decision to change is good for me*
- *I am changing this specific habit (name the habit), now*
- *I can persist until I am successful*

Now you should practice visualizations in which you see yourself successfully overcoming your unwanted habit by discarding the cigarettes, eliminating cookies and ice cream and replacing them with healthy foods, or alternatively, rising punctually in the morning and making the bed. You should perform these affirmations and visualizations regularly and with conviction. But it is well worth it. Once you have experienced the change, you will recognize the value of mobilizing your beliefs to support your actions.

Openness, Love and Self-knowledge

Going with the flow

One of the most profound insights of recent scientific thought is that all things in the known universe are interconnected at the subatomic level. This means that in terms of the universal flow of energy, everything has an impact to some degree on everything else, however small this impact may be. Nothing is ever really isolated or separated. Scientists associated with what is now known as the New Physics regard the universe, and all physical phenomena, as reflecting a dynamic flow of energy and form. They see our world as being made up of an infinite web of interrelationships across the broad spectrum of physical existence, whether we are talking about the bonding of chemical molecules, the relationship between various plant and animal species within an ecosystem, or the relationships between human beings in modern society.

It has become so commonplace to talk in terms of 'going with the flow' that these days it sounds like a cliché. However, the idea of going with the flow actually makes good sense, because it reminds us that the patterns of everyday life have a natural rhythm, and we can be most effective if we are attuned to the flow of events and emotions. Rather than closing ourselves off to this flow –

which really means closing ourselves off to both ourselves and to others – we can seek to be more fluid in our thought patterns and more accepting in our personal way of relating to others.

We can apply this principle of openness and receptivity to ourselves, to those who are only acquaintances, such as people we know mainly from work, or from social or recreational contacts, and to those who are dearest and closest to us: the people we love and care for deeply, and with whom we have an intimate and ongoing connection.

When we consider the concept of openness and receptivity in relation to goals and personal well-being, we must also acknowledge the mutual rights of others who are similarly engaged in related pursuits. At the same time, we can be mindful that each of us has a rich pool of latent talent and creative potential to explore. Although no doubt we live in an increasingly competitive world, we can nevertheless take the decision to explore our capacity for personal growth and development across a broad spectrum of physical, mental, emotional and spiritual goals without it being at the expense of others.

The principle of 'going with the flow' means opening ourselves to the possibility of change, so that even if we begin with very specific goals, we are also open to the possibility that we may gain new insights on our journey of self-discovery, and this in turn will allow us to modify our goals and achieve a more appropriate outcome – an outcome that, perhaps, we hadn't considered initially.

The reverse of this situation is one in which we find ourselves becoming very emotionally driven and fixated on specific goals; this, in turn, becomes a type of closure, in which we are not open to new insights and are actually diminishing our capacity for change. Shakti Gawain's advice for 'going with the flow' is to hold on to personal goals 'lightly,' rather than in a grimly determined fashion, learning to be both firm and flexible.

Here are some positive affirmations for staying open and receptive:

- ❖ *I can relax and let go of my fear*
- ❖ *I am open to new, creative solutions for my life, now*
- ❖ *I can allow myself to go with the flow*

As we saw earlier, we can only make affirmations for ourselves, not for others, because the latter situation really involves what we wish would happen, and is not actually an affirmation at all. Similarly, it is best if we establish our own personal goals, then open ourselves to manifesting these goals in our own lives, without at the same time linking them in some way to what we expect from other people. As the famous Gestalt therapist Fritz Perls once said: 'I am not in this world to live up to your expectations and you are not in this world to live up to mine.' But Perls also recognized our need for connectedness, commenting: 'You are you and I am I, and if by chance we find each other, it's beautiful.'

We have already seen how creative visualization can help us change our beliefs about ourselves, and imprint positive concepts to replace the negative ones that have been holding us back. Creative visualization is also helpful in nurturing and enriching our personal relationships, because it can help us understand the way we feel about ourselves and other people. If, for some deeply held emotional reason, we are closing ourselves off from others by imposing 'mental armor' or some other form of protective barrier, and if we really do want to change that situation, then creative visualization can help us do it. If we want to open ourselves more spontaneously and empathetically to those we love, creative visualization can help with this, too.

Finding out about ourselves

Let's start with you. What sort of a person are you, and how do you see yourself? To develop an authentic sense of self-knowing and to really focus honestly on both your positive and negative attributes, you may find it helpful to write down the following headings on a piece of paper:

- ❖ How I visualize myself (include your physical characteristics, your personality, your way of interacting with others)
- ❖ How I think others see me
- ❖ How others actually see me

Obviously the first two headings relate to your beliefs about yourself, from your own perspective and, theoretically, from the perspective of others who know you. However, the third heading provides you with your 'reality check.'

Ask a few trusted friends and relatives how they actually see you, and how they feel about the way you interact with other people. You may discover a few nice things about yourself you didn't know before!

However, there may also be things you have discovered about yourself that you would now like to change. The next step is to make a list of the things you would like to change in yourself in order of priority. These items can in turn be addressed through positive affirmations relating to the person you wish to become, accompanied by visualizations in which you see yourself successfully making the transition to the 'new you':

- *I accept all my feelings as part of my total being*
- *I am a positive and caring person, now*
- *I respond positively and sympathetically to the thoughts and wishes of others*
- *I deserve to be prosperous and happy*

It is often said that you have to learn to truly love yourself before you can love others. This means accepting yourself as you really are, warts and all, and not simply idealizing yourself or glossing over the defects you know are there but which you would prefer to cover up. Hopefully, when you open yourself up in a loving relationship with another person, your relationship with that person will similarly be based on how they really are, and not on an idealized projection of how you would like to them to be. When you feel you are open to the possibility of giving and receiving love, you may wish to further reinforce this process with a series of affirmations:

✣ *I love who I am*
✣ *I am open to giving love*
✣ *I am open to receiving love*
✣ *I welcome _____ with love (name the person)*
✣ *I offer _____ my love (name the person)*
✣ *I attract happy, loving relationships into my life*

You can of course also combine these affirmations with creative visualization. On the next page is a visualization to help you bring love into your life.

A VISUALIZATION TO ATTRACT LOVE

❤ *Gather some fresh, richly scented flowers – roses, lilac, gardenias or violets are ideal – and place them in a large vase or bowl, thanking them for their gift of life as you do so. Have a small mirror handy nearby, and sit or kneel in front of the bowl of flowers.*

Remove one of the flowers from the bowl, stroking it lovingly over your head and across your face. At the same time, feel that you are opening yourself to the loving energy of the flower. Now close your eyes, brush the flower petals lightly across your eyelids, and say these words:

I see love

❤ *Now, with your eyes still closed, draw the flower down a little and smell its alluring scent. Fill your spirit with its sweet aroma, and say:*

I breathe love

❤ *Now open your eyes, lift the flower above your head, and say:*

I hold love

❤ *Lower the flower so it is near your heart. Stroke it lovingly, feel its spiritual energies merging with yours, and say:*

I feel love

❤ *Now move the flower lower down, press it gently against your stomach, and say:*

I nourish love

💜 Finally, holding the flower in your hand, gaze at your reflection in the mirror, and say these words:

> **Love is before me, Love is behind me**
> **Love is beside me, Love is above me**
> **Love is below me, Love is within me**
> **Love flows from me, Love comes to me**
> **I am loved**

💜 Place the bowl in a location where you can see the flowers frequently, and try to wear the particular flower you have you used in your love visualization. When the flower begins to discolor and wilt, bury it in the ground, thanking it once again for its spiritual blessings. And now adopt a sense of emotional openness so you can truly receive love when it comes, and also be willing to give love in return.

Moving Toward the Spirit

Healing with color

The healing power of color has been known since ancient times. Some colors can have an activating effect on our senses, while other colors are soothing and calming. Some are dynamic and lively, engaging us more with the external world, while other colors speak more to our inner, spiritual realm of awareness.

One of the most effective forms of creative visualization is color breathing, a technique in which you combine color visualization with rhythmic breathing. Color breathing is a way of visualizing different colors entering your body through your breath, in order to enhance your sense of health and vitality.

If we pause for a moment to reflect on the fact that at different times we all carry negative emotions around in our thoughts, we can then understand

that color breathing provides an excellent approach for visualizing renewed well-being and eliminating negativity.

Thoughts arise in our inner world; they have an intangible quality. However, they are nevertheless also very real. As we have seen, our mind constructs our thoughts as part of our perceived experience of the world and our place in it. It is hardly surprising, then, that in modern society, many of our diseases spring directly from what we think and the way we feel, not only about ourselves, but also about other people and the world at large.

As with affirmations, when you practice color breathing, you should focus on the positive rather than the negative, concentrating your awareness on what it is that you specifically want. If you are wishing to revitalize yourself using color breathing, you may find that focusing on red and orange will work well for you, since these are dynamic colors associated with energy and activity. If, on the other hand, you are seeking to overcome pain, breathing in and visualizing blue will definitely help, because it is a soothing, calming color.

Color breathing

First of all, you will need to relax completely, as outlined earlier in this book. Using the table of colors provided here, visualize the color you have selected and allow it to grow in your mind's eye. If the color seems unclear, or begins to blend with another color, persist until the color is pure and true in your inner vision. Now imagine your entire body being bathed in the healing radiance of the color you have chosen. Maintain a pattern of breathing deeply and rhythmically while imagining the color being drawn into your heart center with each inward breath. Now visualize the healing color spreading throughout your body, just below the skin. If there is a particular part of your body which requires healing, visualize the color entering this area and transmitting its healing properties to the part most in need. Then with each outward breath visualize the toxins or disease elements departing from your body, until at last you feel cleansed and purified. End your visualization with a positive affirmation of your health and well-being.

Opposite is a chart that may help you choose the appropriate color for your visualization.

Healing Colors

Red	Stimulant, increases temperature, heartbeat and circulation; use for colds, anaemia, sciatica, rheumatoid arthritis
Orange	Stimulant, activates respiratory system, energises thyroid gland; use for coughs, colds, cramps, or muscle spasms
Yellow	Stimulant, stimulates the mind, relieves lethargy, acts as a tonic; use to decrease mental sluggishness and revitalise the system as a whole
Green	Relaxant, relieves insomnia and irritability, calms nerves; use to relieve exhaustion and inflamed conditions
Blue	Relaxant, relieves inflammation, lowers blood pressure; use for burns, itching, and pain of any kind
Indigo	Relaxant, intuitive color, sedative and pain-relieving qualities; use for treating infections of the eye, ear, and nose
Violet	Relaxant, spiritual color, sedates the mind and nervous system; use to lower the heart rate and to induce sleep

Chakra energy centers

The spiritual tradition of Kundalini yoga identifies seven spiritual energy centers, or chakras, in the body. The ultimate aim of yoga is union with the Higher Self, or Brahman. According to the teachings of Kundalini yoga, a powerful spiritual energy – symbolized as a coiled serpent – lies dormant in the base of the spine. The purpose of Kundalini yoga is to arouse this energy during meditation, then to raise it through each of the chakras in turn. The aim is finally to attain a state of supreme spiritual Oneness, in which our individual consciousness is totally united with the universe.

In the Kundalini yoga tradition, the four lowest chakras are associated with specific colors, and with the elements Earth, Water, Fire, and Air, respectively. The higher chakras are spiritual centers transcending specific colors – they can be visualized most effectively as pure white radiance. Opposite is a table of the seven chakras of Kundalini yoga, with a brief description of their symbolic associations.

The Seven Chakras of Kundalini Yoga

Seventh chakra: Sahasrara
Located on the crown of the head, and associated
with the pineal gland – sometimes referred to as the
'third eye'– Sahasrara is the energy center of
supreme spiritual transcendence

Sixth chakra: Ajna
Located between the eyebrows

Fifth chakra: Visuddha (Spirit)
Located near the Adam's apple in the throat

Fourth chakra: Anahata (Air)
Located near the heart, Anahata is associated
symbolically with love and compassion, and the
breath of new life

Third chakra: Manipura (Fire)
Located just above the navel,
Manipura is associated symbolically with
the fire of sexual passion

Second chakra: Svadisthana (Water)
Located just below the navel, Svadisthana is
associated with the genitals and sexuality

First chakra: Muladhara (Earth)
Located at the base of the spine, Muladhara is
the location of the sleeping Kundalini serpent

As you can see from this table, the first five chakras are linked to specific elements. In the Hindu tradition, these are known as tattvas. You can use your powers of creative visualization to focus your awareness on each of these spiritual centers in turn, awakening the Kundalini energy through the different energy centers of your body. Here are the visualizations for each of the chakras in sequence:

❖ First chakra: a yellow square, representing the element Earth
❖ Second chakra: a horizontal silver crescent with its tips facing upward, representing the element Water
❖ Third chakra: a red triangle, representing the element Fire
❖ Fourth chakra: a blue circle, representing the element Air
❖ Fifth chakra: a black oval, representing Spirit

Once you feel you have mastered the basic visualizations for these five spiritual energy centers, you may wish to seek guidance from a specialist practitioner of Kundalini yoga, since the highest chakras are associated with powerful states of spiritual awakening, and it would be best not to attempt these states of energy arousal by yourself.

Healing music

To help you with your chakra visualizations, you may find
it beneficial to accompany your visualizations with special
selections of ambient music, especially selections that will help
you focus on a particular element, such as Earth, Water, Fire, Air, or Spirit. But
first we must ask ourselves why certain types of music are able to assist the
process of visualization and healing. How does healing music actually work?

Music has therapeutic and healing qualities because of its capacity to
stimulate feelings and associations. Some types of music have a calming,
relaxing quality suitable for alleviating stress, while other forms of music are
intense and dramatic, and help sharpen our awareness or stimulate specific,
well-formed images of association in our mind's eye. Some types of music
create a sense of harmony and balance, while other discordant forms of music
might leave us restless, on edge, or lacking resolution. Some styles of music
may seem to us to be trivial or whimsical, while other musical compositions
have a deep and enriching impact that is profound or inspiring.

When choosing selections of music for visualization or relaxation, it is
important that you should test the music first, to ensure that it evokes the
specific associations you are seeking. Like a positive affirmation, your selection
of music should help reinforce a particular focus or goal: in this case, the target
is the visualization image and its associations. If the music you have chosen
begins to compete with your visualization, the value of the music is obviously
greatly reduced, and the music may actually become a negative factor.

Selections of music chosen for the element Spirit are usually also suitable
as ambient backgrounds for relaxation and general meditation. Such music is
typically devoid of strong melodic content, and opens us to a state of expanded
awareness while also remaining gentle and reflective. It is music which literally
enhances our inner journey of the spirit.

Here is a selection of music for relaxation and visualization. Of course, the
final choice is entirely up to you!

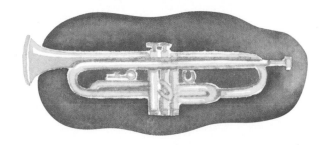

Music for relaxation and visualization

Music for the spirit

- ❖ Aeoliah and Larkin, *Inner Sanctum* (Celestial Octaves)
- ❖ Aeoliah and Mike Rowland, 'The Healing Heart' and 'We are One Light,' from *The Reiki Effect* (Oreade)
- ❖ Ash Ra, 'Ocean of Tenderness,' from *New Age of Earth* (Virgin)
- ❖ Harold Budd and Brian Eno, *The Pearl* (EG / Polygram)
- ❖ *Ambient One: Music for Airports* (EG/Polygram)
- ❖ *Ambient Two: The Plateaux of Mirror* (EG/Polygram)
- ❖ Deuter, 'Green Mandala' from *Sun Spirit* (New Earth)
- ❖ Brian Eno, *Thursday Afternoon* (EG/Polygram)
- ❖ Steven Halpern, *Eventide* (Halpern Sounds)
- ❖ *Zodiac Suite* (Halpern Sounds)
- ❖ Nancy Hennings and Henry Wolff, *Tibetan Bells* and *Tibetan Bells II* (Celestial Harmonies)
- ❖ Gyorgy Ligeti, 'Requiem' and 'Lux Aeterna,' from the 2001 soundtrack (MGM)
- ❖ Ray Lynch, *The Sky of Mind* (Windham Hill)

Music for visualizing the elements

Earth

- ❖ Deuter, *Ecstasy* (Kuckuk)
- ❖ Brian Eno, *Ambient Four: On Land* (EG/Polygram)
- ❖ Steven Halpern, 'In the Hall of Records,' 'Trippin,' and 'Udu Blue,' from *Deja Blues* (Halpern's Inner Peace Music)
- ❖ Kitaro, *Oasis* (Kuckuk) and 'Harmony of the Forest,' from *Thinking of You* (Domo)

Water

- ❖ Brian Eno and Harold Budd, *Ambient Two: The Plateaux of Mirror* (EG/Polygram)
- ❖ Pink Floyd, 'Echoes,' from *Meddle* (Harvest/EMI)
- ❖ Fripp and Eno, *Evening Star* (Island)
- ❖ Edgar Froese, *Aqua* (Virgin)
- ❖ Kitaro, 'Spirit of Water,' from *Thinking of You* (Domo)

Fire

- ❖ Ash Ra, 'Sun Rain,' from *New Age of Earth* (Virgin)
- ❖ Philip Glass, 'The Grid,' from *Koyaanisqatsi* (Island)
- ❖ Laraaji, *Ambient Three: Day of Radiance* (EG/Polygram)

Air

- ❖ Aeoliah and Mike Rowland, 'Twin Flames Rising,' from *The Reiki Effect* (Oreade)
- ❖ Brian Eno, 'Under Stars' and 'Weightless,' from *Apollo* (EG/Polygram)
- ❖ Fripp and Eno, 'Wind on Water' and 'Wind on Wind,' from *Evening Star* (Island)
- ❖ Paul Horn, *Inside the Great Pyramid* (Mushroom)

Now that you have made your selections of ambient music, you may like to try a healing visualization. This one should be accompanied by music you have chosen for spirit:

A HEALING VISUALIZATION WITH MUSIC

❖ *As the music begins, breathe deeply, relaxing in a way that works for you.*

❖ *Visualize yourself standing in a field of flowers. Feel the sun warming your head and shoulders, and become aware of a gentle breeze fanning your cheek as you look around the field. Spend a few moments becoming aware of yourself standing in the sun-drenched field. Now begin to breathe gently and deeply, imagining that the air you breathe in is filled with sparkling white light and that this white light is being drawn into your body. Then, as you breathe out, notice the cloudiness as the breath from your body meets the outside air beyond. Imagine this outward breath carrying with it any negative elements you wish to expel from your body. Spend a few moments breathing in this way until your breath becomes clear and any impurities have departed from your body.*

❖ *See yourself turning in the center of the field. Now you discover a large clear bubble and you feel yourself moving into the center of this bubble. You stand there comfortably as the bubble surrounds you completely. Now the bubble begins to rise up into the air, and soon you are suspended in space.*

❖ *Now you are floating freely, higher and higher, and as you do, you begin to feel your whole body being revitalized; every cell in your body is now in perfect health. Spend a little time experiencing this state of purity and health.*

❖ *Now your bubble gently begins to return to earth, landing softly in the center of the field of flowers. As you emerge from the bubble, you notice that you are now exactly as you would ideally like to be. It is as if the old you went up in the bubble and has been transformed into a totally new, revitalized and healthy human being. Feel the vibration of this new healthy being flow through every cell in your body as you remain quiet and relaxed, allowing the music to flow through you.*

Contacting your inner guides

Many people like to practice a form of visualization that involves contacting their inner guides. You may regard your inner guides as personifications of your inner self or higher spiritual potential, or you may think of them as external beings – like angels or spirits – who intercede on your behalf to heighten your powers of intuition or bring you wisdom and inspiration. They can be male or female, or figures from the ancient, mythic past. They can be familiar, or eccentric and unconventional. The important point is to trust that your inner guide can bring to your realm of conscious awareness insights and information that you will find useful in your everyday life, information that probably would not have become available to you through more familiar and conventional processes.

However we regard them, inner guides exist in a realm beyond our direct conscious awareness. Nevertheless, we can use our powers of creative visualization to make contact with them! Opposite is a visualization for contacting your inner guide.

CONTACTING YOUR INNER GUIDE

❖ *Close your eyes and enter a state of deep relaxation using the techniques described earlier in this book. Now visualize that you are journeying on a path toward a special, sacred place. It is a place that is safe and secret – a place known only to you.*

❖ *Now, as you venture further along this path, you notice a figure in the distance, coming toward you. The figure shines with radiant light, emanating a feeling of tranquillity and deep knowing – and you realize that this is your inner guide. As your guide comes closer, you are able to tell whether this figure is male or female. You also take note of the garments this person is wearing, whether the being is young or old, and other distinctive aspects of his or her external appearance.*

❖ *Greet your guide, ask for the guide's name, and then proceed together to your special, sacred place. When you arrive, show your guide around, explain why this place is sacred to you, and make him or her feel welcome. Then ask your guide some specific questions or inquire whether there is something he or she wishes to impart to you. Some answers may be forthcoming immediately, but if not, don't panic. Your questions will be answered later.*

❖ *When the meeting with your guide seems to have reached some form of conclusion, thank this figure of light, ask him or her to make contact with you again in the future, and make your way back down the path to your familiar everyday world. When you feel ready, open your eyes ...*

❖ *Your inner guide is a special being whom you may call on whenever you are in need of special insights, intuition, wisdom, or loving advice. You may wish to keep a diary to note down the insights or intuitions you receive from your inner guide, and also to keep a record of how you have applied these wisdom lessons in your everyday life.*

Achieving Total Well-being

Creative visualization for health and vitality

Earlier in this book, we described the visualization process for awakening the Kundalini energy by focusing on the different chakras of the body. That process was based on the idea of raising your conscious awareness up to the level of spiritual Oneness – the level of total mystical transcendence. However, it is also possible to draw the sacred life-giving energies of the universe down into your body; this is an ideal visualization to help you restore your overall sense of health and vitality.

Try the visualization opposite as a way of purifying your body and regaining your sense of mental and spiritual well-being.

AWAKENING THE ENERGY CENTERS FROM ABOVE

❧ *Sit down in a chair in a comfortable, meditative position, with your back straight and your hands resting in your lap. Close your eyes and breathe deeply, so that you are completely relaxed. Now visualize a ball of radiant white light immediately above your head. Imagine that this ball of light represents the pure spiritual light of the Universe – the light of true healing – and that it is about to descend into the crown of your head.*

❧ *Breathe deeply in and out, now visualizing this ball of light descending into your head, radiating health and vitality in all directions.*

❧ *Now watch with your mind's eye as you draw this ball of light down into your throat. Continue to breathe in and out, deeply and regularly, as you absorb the healing radiance into this part of your body.*

❧ *Visualize the ball of light descending still further, until it comes down into your chest. You feel now as if your body is truly lit from within, and a wonderful healing radiance extends to all regions of your chest. As you breathe in you feel the reawakening of vitality, and as you breathe out, you feel that you are expelling any impurities or toxins that have been restricting your health and well-being until this moment of release.*

❧ *And now you draw the ball of light down still further so that it radiates its healing light just above your navel. When you have filled this region with light, bring the sphere down just below your navel, and then in turn draw it down into your pelvic region. Once again, feel the nurturing, restorative power of the light as it fills your body with its healing radiance.*

❧ *Finally, imagine that this healing sphere of light has now reached down to your feet, grounding itself and vibrating like a pulse through the very core of your being. You feel deeply relaxed, and profoundly purified. The healing light now dwells fully within you.*

❧ *Give thanks for this gift of light and, when you are ready, open your eyes and return to the everyday reality of your familiar surroundings.*

Controlling pain

All of us, at some time in our lives, have felt the debilitating and agonizing effects of pain in our bodies. Maybe we are prone to headaches or migraines, or perhaps we have experienced pain as the result of physical injury. Fortunately, it is possible to reduce the effects of pain through creative visualization, although it should not be regarded as an alternative to medical treatment. Rather, we can think of creative visualization as an additional tool for targeting the cause of pain and helping reduce its impact.

It will help if we pause for a moment to consider the nature of pain itself. First, pain involves tensing your muscles. If one part of your body is in pain, you tense the muscles elsewhere in your body in an effort to favor that painful spot. As we have seen, relaxation helps remove tension, so that is the first step toward a positive response.

Second, it is worth remembering that the pain you are feeling is in your brain, not in the localized part of your body that is hurt. If you have a sore arm, the pain of that sore arm is in your brain, and the intensity of the pain depends on the response of your brain to the messages it is receiving via your nerves and spinal cord en route to the brain itself. Your brain produces chemical neurotransmitters (natural opiates known as endorphins) that are capable of preventing further pain messages being transmitted back to your brain.

Creative visualization can be used to block pain messages. When you practice creative visualization, your brain automatically creates alpha and theta brain waves, which enhance your capacity to create pain-blocking neurotransmitters. Visualization can also help you focus on the psychological and emotional aspects of your pain, which may also be contributing to its impact.

It is often said that pain serves as a measure of the resistance we have in our internal system. Some initial questions we can ask if we experience pain are: What am I resisting? Am I truly going with the flow and following the stream of life awareness, or am I fighting against its current? Is there something I can do in my day-to-day life that will help lessen the pain I am inflicting on myself?

The next time you suffer from a headache, for example, rather than reaching for a pill, you may find it a good idea to direct your awareness into the specific area of the pain. As a first step, imagine what shape this pain takes in your body. Picture the shape clearly, and begin to visualize its color and texture. Next, become aware of the taste or smell of the shape, then imagine that the shape is riding on the back of a wave of sound. Now release this wave of sound, watching as the shape flies away in the distance. This simple visualization, especially if repeated a few times, will help remove most general pains.

Let's say, though, that you have a more persistent headache, a headache that simply refuses to go away. You can begin by focusing clearly on the pain. Where exactly is the pain? Try to locate it specifically in your body, even to the nearest millimeter! Where exactly is it located?

Having located the exact position or source of the pain, you can now begin to visualize its shape and size. Do you see it as round or square, pointed or elongated – or some other shape? Is it ragged, sharp or smooth? What color is it? Finally, does it have a smell or suggest a taste? Once you have focused on your pain in this way, you should try to imagine what sensation it would provide if it were located somewhere else in your body. Try moving it to another position in your head; then try moving it to another location in your body, such as your knee, ankle, or shoulder.

Now you can try moving it outside your body altogether, so that it is completely out of sight and mind. If you are successful at visualizing the release of your pain in this way, you will soon find that the pain diminishes, then finally disappears totally.

Getting in touch with your 'inner doctor'

As we have already seen, our mind and body are closely interrelated, and the way in which we think plays an important role in our state of well-being. So it follows that positive mental images can lead to a healthy lifestyle, complementing healthy dietary and exercise routines.

Once again, you can use creative visualization to get in touch with your true overall state of health. Sit down, relax and take a few deep breaths in and out, using all the visualization skills you have already learned. Now allow your mental awareness to travel slowly across every part of your body. As it does so, make a mental note of how each part of your body feels to you. As noted earlier, there may be spots of tension. Let go of this tension if you can. Picture your state of health in a total sense. How does your body look to you, and how do you feel inside? Does any tell-tale imagery arise at this time? Do any warning images arise in your awareness – images that seem to be at variance with how you ideally see yourself? Has it become clear that you will have to make some adjustments to your diet or physical habits in order to regain a true state of health and well-being? If you recognize these necessary changes and are willing to act on them, you can now use visualization to see yourself doing the things that will help make you well. At the same time, you can imagine how it feels to make these changes in your lifestyle and really benefit from them. In time, a healthier image of you – a really healthier you – will emerge and become a reality.

For example, if you are concerned that you are overweight, visualize yourself standing in front of a mirror admiring the sort of physical shape you would really like to have. Now form a plan of action and visualize the necessary steps that you will need to undergo in order to attain this ideal body shape. If you are a smoker, visualize yourself as a person who has successfully quit the habit. Explore the fresher taste and smell sensations in your mouth and on your breath. Notice how your food tastes so much better. Visualize your bronchial passages free of all that cigarette tar. See yourself radiating health, with more color in your complexion and a bounce in your step. Congratulate yourself for having overcome a health-debilitating habit!

Finally, in the same way that you have become used to contacting your inner guides, you may also wish to get in touch more regularly with your 'inner doctor.' In your own sacred and private space, the same place you have been going to meet your inner guides, visualize meetings with a healer or physician whom you can trust completely to provide you with the sort of guidance and expertise you require. Listen carefully to the answers which your inner doctor gives you, for your body/mind system has its own innate wisdom; often you will be able to obtain valuable insights from your own intuitive resources.

Remember: your thoughts help create your reality

If you are going through a period of illness, you may want to use creative visualization to reinforce a mental image of how healthy you were before you got sick, and how healthy you are now becoming as you emerge from your illness. In this regard, it may also help to visualize your disease as a shape or object, then subsequently to visualize your treatment invading and conquering your 'disease-object,' thus eliminating it altogether.

The insights you receive through creative visualization should, of course, be carefully considered in relation to any conventional medical treatment you are receiving, and are not intended as a substitute. However, you may be surprised to discover that your mind and body may already know what is good for you, if only your personal belief system could allow it to happen!

Remember our starting point – your thoughts help create your reality. What you believe about yourself has a very real impact on your state of well-being. Make a practice of visualizing yourself as a person who is healthy and well, so you can manifest this as a reality in your everyday life!

The greatest discovery of my life is that a human being can
alter his life by altering his attitude.

William James

Glossary

Active meditation another name for creative visualization. Some forms of 'passive' Eastern meditation seek to eliminate imagery from conscious awareness. 'Active meditation' uses the emotive and sensory impact of visual imagery.

Affirmation a concise, accurate statement describing a personal goal (sometimes known also as a positive affirmation).

Ambient music non-intrusive music conceived for relaxation, meditation or visualization.

Belief-system a cluster of personal beliefs. Such belief systems may be either positive or negative.

Brahman in Hinduism, the supreme reality in the universe. Brahman is more than God, more than Spirit. Brahman is totally beyond definition – the Absolute.

Chakras in Kundalini yoga, spiritual energy centers aligned with the central nervous column in the human body. The seven chakras, from lowest to highest, are Muladhara, Svadisthana, Manipura, Anahata, Visuddha, Ajna and Sahasrara.

Color breathing a technique of visualization in which healing light of a specific and appropriate color is breathed into the body in order to produce a healing response.

Color healing any form of healing that draws on the healing qualities of different colored light.

Imagination the capacity of the mind to produce images through the various senses.

Imprinting the act of implanting a decision for change both externally (through actions) and internally (by changing one's personal beliefs).

Inner guide a helper figure from the inner realm who can be contacted via a state of visionary consciousness.

Left hemisphere the hemisphere of the brain associated with analytical and logical thought, with verbal and written communication, and with mathematical concepts.

Manifesting the act of attracting into our life something which we really want. Creative visualization and positive affirmations are both ways of manifesting.

Positive affirmation see Affirmation.

Progressive relaxation a form of relaxation in which different parts of the body are relaxed progressively: that is, in sequence.

Right hemisphere the hemisphere of the brain associated with spatial relationships and wholes. It is also the region of the brain associated with intuition, emotion, passion, creativity, visual imagery and dreams.

Tattvas Hindu symbols of the five elements. The tattvas are Prithivi (yellow square: Earth); Apas (silver crescent: Water); Tejas (red triangle: Fire); Vayu (blue circle: Air); and Akasha (black oval/egg: Spirit).

Tense-and-release muscle relaxation a form of relaxation exercise in which different parts of the body are tensed up and then allowed to relax, thereby releasing tension from the body one section at a time.

Further Reading

Dyer, Wayne, *Real Magic*, HarperCollins, New York, 1992.

Fanning, Patrick, *Visualization for Change*, New Harbinger Publications, Oakland, California, 1988.

Fezler, William, *Creative Imagery*, Simon & Schuster, New York, 1989.

Gawain, Shakti, *Creative Visualization*, Whatever Publishing, Mill Valley, California, 1978.

Gawler, Ian, *The Creative Power of Imagery*, Hill of Content, Melbourne, 1997.

Jacobson, Edmund, *Progressive Relaxation*, University of Chicago Press, Chicago, 1942.

Markham, Ursula, *The Elements of Visualisation*, Element Books, Dorset, 1989.

Samuels, Mike and Nancy, *Seeing with the Mind's Eye*, Random House, New York, 1975.

Shone, Ronald, *Creative Visualization*, Thorsons, London, 1984.

Simonton, Carl (et al), *Getting Well Again*, Bantam, New York, 1980.

Steinbrecher, Edwin C., *The Inner Guide Meditation*, Weiser, Maine, 1988.

Watson, Andrew and Drury, Nevill, *Healing Music*, Prism Press, Dorset, 1987.

This edition published by Barnes & Noble, Inc.,
by arrangement with Lansdowne Publishing

2001 Barnes & Noble Books

ISBN 0-7607-2763-5

M 10 9 8 7 6 5 4 3 2 1

Commissioned by Deborah Nixon
Production Manager: Sally Stokes
Text: Nevill Drury
Designer: Avril Makula
Editor: Patti Dacey
Illustrator: Sue Ninham
Project Coordinator: Kate Merrifield

Set in Revival on QuarkXPress
Printed in Singapore by Tien Wah Press (Pte) Ltd